Hooked on Golf!

Great Quotations Publishing Co.

Compiled by: Julie Otlewis
Cover Art & Inside Illustration by: Quinn Kanecko
Typeset and Design by: Julie Otlewis

© 1993 Great Quotations Publishing Company

All rights reserved.
Written permission must be secured from the publisher
to use or reproduce any part of this book,
except for brief quotations in critical reviews or articles.

Published by Great Quotations Publishing Company
1967 Quincy Court
Glendale Heights, Illinois 60139

Printed in Hong Kong

Always throw clubs ahead of you. That way you don't have to waste energy going back to pick them up.

— *Tommy Bolt*

Putting isn't golf.
Greens should be treated almost
the same as water hazards:
you land on them, then add
two strokes to your score.

— Chi Chi Rodriguez

Actually, the only time I ever took out a
one-iron was to kill a tarantula.
And I took a seven to do that.

— Jim Murray

Gimme: an agreement between
two losers who can't putt.

— Jim Bishop

You can hit a 2-acre fairway
10% of the time,
and a 2-inch branch
90% of the time.

The players themselves can be
classified into two groups -
the attractions and the entry fees.

— *Jimmy Demaret*

Golf is the hardest game in the world
to play and the easiest to cheat at.

— Dave Hill

Let's face it, ninety-five percent
of this game is mental.
A guy plays lousy golf, he doesn't
need a pro, he needs a shrink.

— Tom Murphy

What's over there?
A nudist colony?

*— Lee Trevino, after his three playing partners
drove into the woods*

Many a husband has a secret craving
to use his golf clubs in a way the
manufacturer didn't intend.

I've seen lifelong friends drift apart over golf just because one could play better, but the other counted better.

— Stephen Leacock

My worst day on the golf course
still beats my best day in the office.

The only time I talk on a golf course is to my caddie - and only then to complain.

— *Seve Ballesteros*

As of this writing, there are approximately 2,450 reasons why a person hits a rotten shot, and more are being discovered every day.

— Jay Cronley

If the wind is in your face, you swing
too hard just to get the ball through it;
if the wind is at your back,
you swing too hard just to see how
far you can get the ball to go.

The shortest distance between any two points on a golf course is a straight line that passes directly through the center of a very large tree.

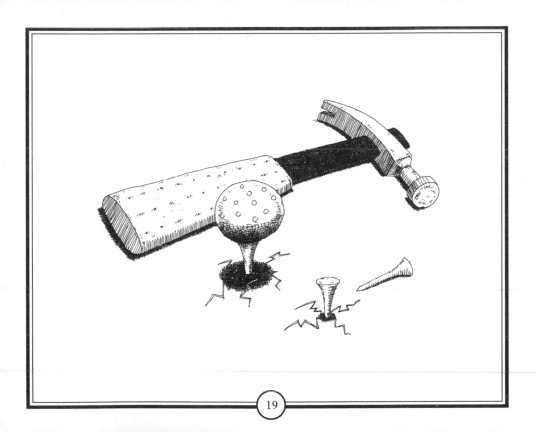

If you break 100,
watch your golf.
If you break 80,
watch your business.

— Joey Adams

Golf is a game in which
the slowest people in the world are
those in front of you, and the fastest
are those behind.

If you watch a game,
it's fun.
If you play it,
it's recreation.
If you work at it, it's golf.

— Bob Hope

Don't play with anyone who would question a 7.

Never take lessons from your father,
teach golf to your wife or
play your son for money!

Have you ever noticed what
golf spells backwards?

— Al Boliska

The best thing that can be said about golf is that it isn't compulsory.

The man who takes up golf to get his mind off his work, soon takes up work to get his mind off golf.

Golf: A day spent in a round
of strenuous idleness.

— *William Wordsworth*

You've just one problem.
You stand too close to the ball -
after you've hit it.

— Sam Snead, to a pupil

I have three-putted in
over forty countries.

— Fred Corcoran

If profanity had an influence on the flight of the ball, the game would be played far better than it is.

— *Horace G. Hutchinson*

Golf is a game whose aim is to hit a very small ball into an even smaller hole, with weapons singularly ill-designed for the purpose.

— Winston Churchill

A beginner's golf game is improving when he is able to hit the ball in one.

The man who never falls asleep
in church on Sunday is probably
out on the golf course.

It took me seventeen years to get
three thousand hits in baseball.
I did it in one afternoon on
the golf course.

— Hank Aaron

When you look up and cause an awful shot, you will always look down again at exactly the moment when you ought to start watching the ball if you ever want to see it again.

Many a golfer prefers a golf cart to a caddy because it cannot count, criticize - or laugh.

The statute of limitations
on forgotten strokes
is two holes.

All truly great golf courses have an almost supernatural finishing hole, by way of separating the chokers from the strokers.

— Charles Price

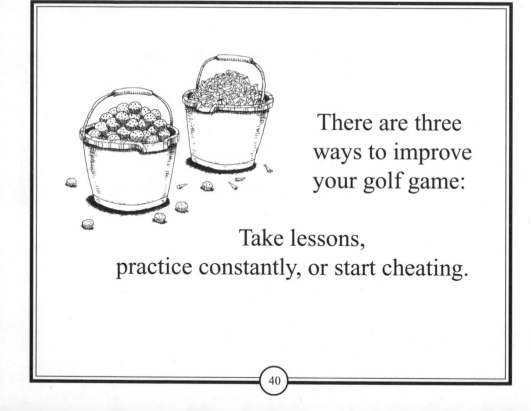

There are three ways to improve your golf game:

Take lessons,
practice constantly, or start cheating.

If you think it's hard to meet
new people try picking up
the wrong golf ball.

— Jack Lemmon

The good thing about golf is that you can be a pedestrian without being run over.

I play in the low 80's.
If it's any hotter than that,
I won't play.

– Joe E. Lewis

When I first came out on tour,
I swung all out on every tee shot.
My drives finished so far off line,
my pants were grass-stained .
at the knees.

— Fuzzy Zoeller

Golf and sex are about the only things
you can enjoy without being good at it.

— Jimmy Demaret

Real golfers don't use naked-lady tees.

As soon as
a businessman
takes up golf,
he becomes
an executive.

It's good sportsmanship to not pick up lost golf balls while they are still rolling.

— *Mark Twain*

In golf and in life,
it's the follow through that
makes the difference.

For most amateurs,
the best wood in the bag
is the pencil.

— *Chi Chi Rodriguez*

I'd give up golf if I didn't have
so many sweaters.

— Bob Hope

Another thing to be thankful for is that many people do their worst driving on the golf courses.

Making a hole in one isn't
so wonderful - look at all
the exercise you miss.

I'm hitting the woods just great,
but I'm having a terrible time
getting out of them.

— Harry Tofcano

A lot of guys who have never choked,
have never been in the position
to do so.

— Tom Watson

The best way to get a man to dig in a garden would be to call it a sand trap.

The only shots you can be dead sure of
are those you've had already.

— Byron Nelson

Teach your wife to play golf,
and she'll never hit anything;
teach her to drive a car,
and she'll never miss.

I was on the dance floor,
but I couldn't hear the band.

— Chi Chi Rodriguez,
on a fifty foot putt

The harder you work,
the luckier you get.

— *Gary Player*

Golf is an awkward set of bodily
contortions designed to produce a
graceful result.

— *Tommy Armour*

There's nothing like golf to build a man
up physically and mentally so that
he can play more golf.

Hook: the addiction of
fifty percent of all golfers.
Slice: the weakness of
the other half.

— Jim Bishop

Never bet with anyone you meet on
the first tee who has a deep suntan,
a one-iron in his bag and squinty eyes.

— Dave Marr

I still swing the way I used to,
but when I look up, the ball is going
in a different direction.

— Lee Trevino

The golf swing is like sex.
You can't be thinking about the
mechanics of the act
while you're performing.

— *Dave Hill*

When you're too old to
chase other things,
you can always chase golf balls.

An amateur golfer is one who
addresses the ball twice -
before and after swinging.

Everybody has two swings:
the one he uses during the
last three holes of a tournament and
the one he uses the rest of the time.

— *Toney Penna*

When I'm on a course and it
starts to rain and lightning,
I hold up my one iron, 'cause I know
even God can't hit a one iron.

— Lee Trevino

Golf was once a rich man's sport,
but it now has millions of poor players.

Mulligan:
invented by an Irishman who
wanted to hit one more
twenty yard grounder.

— *Jim Bishop*

There's an old saying:
If a man comes home with sand in his
cuffs and cockleburs in his pants,
don't ask him what he shot.

— *Sam Snead*

The best time to visit the driving range
is at night when you can
hardly see the ball.

— Stephen Baker

Golf is a game in which
you yell 'fore', shoot six,
and write down five.

— Paul Harvey

Statistics indicate that,
as a result of overwork, modern
executives are dropping like flies on
the nation's golf courses.

— Ira Wallach

If you drink, don't drive.
Don't even putt.

— *Dean Martin*

Golf is an easy game...
it's just hard to play.

No matter how early your tee time, there will always be a foursome in the middle of the first fairway.

Nothing goes down slower than
a golf handicap.

— Bobby Nichols

They say that trees are no problem
because trees are ninety percent air.

— John Brodie

Your financial cost can best be figured out when you realize that if you were to devote the same time and energy to business instead of golf, you would be a millionaire in approximately six weeks.

— *Buddy Hackett*

You don't know what pressure is
until you play for five bucks
with only two in your pocket.

— *Lee Trevino*

The greater the bet, the longer the short putts become.

Hell is standing on the most beautiful golf course that's ever been made and not having a set of clubs.

— Jim Meyers

A golfer is a man who keeps his elbow
straight for eighteen holes,
but bends it on the nineteenth.

It takes 17 holes to really get warmed up.

Your straightest iron shot
of the day will be
exactly one club short.

I didn't need to finish college to know what golf was all about. All you need to know is to hit the ball, find it and hit it again until it disappears into the hole in the ground.

— Fuzzy Zoeller

The consolation for the loser in golf is that he gets more practice and exercise than the winner; he gets to hit the ball more times.

The practice putting green is either half
as fast or twice as fast as all
the other greens.

The fun you get from golf is in direct ratio to the effort you don't put into it.

— Bob Allen

If you're stupid enough to whiff,
you should be smart enough to forget it.

— Arnold Palmer

I spent so much time in the rough,
my playing partner Buddy Allin
thought I was part of the gallery.

— Lee Trevino

I can't believe the actions of some of our top pros. They should have side jobs modeling for Pampers.

— Fuzzy Zoeller

There is no movement in the golf swing so difficult that it cannot be made even more difficult by careful study and diligent practice.

There are no short hitters on tour anymore - just long and unbelievably long.

— *Sam Snead*

I owe everything to golf.
Where else could a guy with an IQ
like mine make this much money?

— Hubert Green

The number of tees in your bag is always less than 3 or more than 600.

If you ever par the first three holes, you'll have a 20 minute wait on the fourth tee.

Golfers don't fist fight.
They cuss a lot. But they wouldn't punch
anything or anybody. They might hurt
their hands and have to change their grip.

— Dan Jenkins

I never pray on the golf course.
Actually, the Lord answers my prayers
everywhere except on the course.

— Rev. Billy Graham

Progress in golf consists of two steps forward, and 26.6 miles backward.

Nonchalant putts count the same
as chalant putts.

My putter had a heart attack the last nine holes and just died on me.

— Lanny Wadkins, after leading for three rounds and slipping to fourth.

Golf is the most fun you can have
without taking your clothes off.

— Chi Chi Rodriguez

Nobody ever looked up
and saw a good shot.

— *Don Herold*

Greater love hath no man that this - that he give up his golf for his wife.

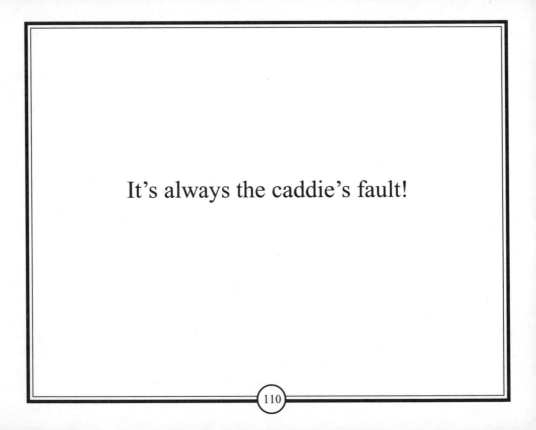

It's always the caddie's fault!

If I'da cleared the trees and drove the green, it woulda been a great tee shot.

— Sam Snead

Golf isn't so much a
game as a passionate faith that you can
hit it a mile next time.

The game of golf is 90% mental
and 10% mental.

It's as easy to lower your handicap as it is to reduce your hat size.

If you really want to get better at golf,
go back and take it up at a
much earlier age.

Whatever you leave out of your bag is the one thing you will need - if it is Band-aids, you will develop a blister; if it is a spare glove, yours will tear on the fifth hole.

Golf combines two favorite American pastimes: taking long walks and hitting things with a stick.

— P.J. O'Rourke

If it really made sense to "let the club do the work," you'd just say, "Driver, wedge to the green, one-putt," and walk to the next tee.

It's a simple matter to keep your ball in the fairway if you're not too choosy about which fairway.

A cardinal rule for the
club breaker is never to break your
putter and driver in the same match
or you are dead.

— *Tommy Bolt*

The only thing of real value that you can take from the driving range to the first tee is a pocketful of range balls.

Never try to keep more than 300 separate thoughts in your mind during your swing.

The secret of good golf is to hit the ball hard, straight, and not too often.

Golf is a game where guts,
stick-to-it-iveness and blind devotion
will always net you absolutely
nothing but an ulcer.

— *Tommy Bolt*

I only hit the ball about 220 off the tee,
but I can always find it.

— Bonnie Lauer

I've thrown or broken a few clubs in my day. In fact, I guess at one time or another I probably held distance records for every club in the bag.

— Tommy Bolt

It is a law of nature that everybody
plays a hole badly when going through.

— Bernard Darwin

I may be the only golfer never
to have broken a single putter,
if you don't count the one I twisted into
a loop and threw into a bush.

— *Thomas Boswell*

Real golfers don't cry
when they line up their fourth putt.

Every day I try to tell myself this is going to be fun today. I try to put myself in a great frame of mind before I go out, then I screw it up with the first shot.

— *Johnny Miller*

Golf is a nonviolent game played
violently from within.

— Bob Toski

I never did see the sense in keeping my head down. The only reason I play golf at all is to see where the ball goes.

— *Charles Price*

Knowing the swing weight of your club is as indispensable to playing good golf as knowing the temperature of the grass in the fairway.

The only reason
I ever played golf
in the first place
was so I could
afford to hunt
and fish.

— Sam Snead

After taking the stance, it is too late to worry. The only thing to do then is to hit the ball.

— *Bobby Jones*

The secret of golf is, use your real swing to take the big divot, use your practice swing to make the shot, and always hit the do-over first.

The stages of a
golfer's game are:
Sudden Collapse,
Radical Change,
Complete Frustration,
Slow Improvement,
Brief Mastery, and
Sudden Collapse.

I buried a few in the ground, you know.
It took two men to get one of them out.

— Dave Hill

Strokes always accumulate faster than they can be forgotten.

Golf does strange things to other people, too. It makes liars out of honest men, cheats out of altruists, cowards out of brave men and fools out of everybody.

— *Milton Gross*

No matter how
badly you are
playing,
it is always
possible to
play worse.

He was standing
too close to my ball.

*— Barry M. Goldwater, after beaning a spectator
thirty yards off the tee.*

This is the hardest game in the world, believe me. There is no way a golfer can think he is really something, because that's when the game gets you.

— Ben Crenshaw

Golf is like art;
it's impossible to be perfect.

— *Sandra Palmer*

Since bad shots come in groups of three, a fourth bad shot is actually the beginning of the next group of three.

When your shot has to carry over a water hazard, you can either hit one more club or two more balls.

My game is so bad I gotta hire
three caddies - one to walk the left rough,
one for the right rough, and one down
the middle. And the one in the middle
doesn't have much to do.

— Dave Hill

There's no game like golf; you go out with three strangers, play eighteen holes, and return with three enemies.

In life, a man's honesty is often his handicap: in golf, a man's handicap is often his honesty.

Great golf courses should have
at least one silly hole.

— Frank Hannigan

In primitive society, when native tribes beat the ground with clubs and yell, it is called witchcraft; in civilized society it is called golf.

In golf, nothing counts like
your opponent.

Sometimes a golfer makes such a wild shot that when he finally finds the ball, he has lost the course.

Golf matches are not won on the fairways or greens. They are won on the tee - the first tee.

Give me a banana.
I'm playing like a monkey.
I might as well eat like one.

— Chi Chi Rodriguez

No golfer ever played too fast!

Baffling late-life discovery:
Golfers wear those awful clothes
on purpose.

— Herb Caen

The longer you play, the better chance
the better player has of winning.

— Jack Nicklaus

The more often your opponent quotes the rules, the greater the certainty that he cheats.

The only time you play great golf is when you are doing everything within your power to lose to your boss.

My goal this year is basically to
find the fairways.

— Lauri Peterson

A ball hit to the wrong green will always land two feet from the hole.

Never, never, never, never, will I ever be able to force myself to hit a pink golf ball. After all, the line has to be drawn somewhere.

— Peter Dobereiner

It's often necessary to hit a second drive to really appreciate the first one.

It always takes
at least five holes
to notice that a
club is missing.

Willis' Rule of Golf:
You can't lose an old golf ball.

— John Willis

Don't buy a putter until you've had
a chance to throw it.

OTHER TITLES BY GREAT QUOTATIONS PUBLISHING COMPANY

199 Useful Things to Do With A Politician
201 Best Things Ever Said
A Lifetime of Love
A Light Heart Lives Long
A Teacher Is Better Than Two Books
As A Cat Thinketh
Cheatnotes On Life
Chicken Soup
Dear Mr. President
Father Knows Best
Food For Thought
Golden Years, Golden Words
Happiness Walks On Busy Feet
Heal The World
Hooked on Golf
Hollywords

In Celebration of Women
Life's Simple Pleasures
For Mother - A Bouquet of Sentiment
Motivation Magic
Mrs. Webster's Dictionary
I'm Not Over The Hill ...
Reflections
Romantic Rendezvous
Sports Page
So Many Ways To Say Thank You
The ABC's of Parenting
The Best Of Friends
The Birthday Astrologer
The Little Book of Spiritual Wisdom
Things You'll Learn, If You Live Long Enough

GREAT QUOTATIONS PUBLISHING CO.

1967 Quincy Court
Glendale Heights, IL 60139-2045
Phone (708) 582-2800
FAX (708) 582-2813